# President Donald Trump

JOANNE MATTERN

**Children's Press**®
An Imprint of Scholastic Inc.

**Content Consultant**
James Marten, PhD
Professor and Chair, History Department
Marquette University
Milwaukee, Wisconsin

Cataloging-in-Publication Data is available online at https://lccn.loc.gov

Front cover: Donald Trump
Back cover: Donald Trump at inauguration

# Find the Truth!

**Everything** you are about to read is true *except* for one of the sentences on this page.

Which one is **TRUE**?

**T or F**    Trump's father was a real estate developer.

**T or F**    Trump ran for president of the United States for the first time in 2016.

Find the answers in this book.

# Contents

Donald, Barron,
and Melania Trump

4

Trump at an event for *The Apprentice*

**THE BIG TRUTH!**

## Counting the Vote

Who really votes for president? . . . . . . . . . . **40**

Trump on the campaign trail

Donald Trump (center) sits in the President's Room in the U.S. Capitol, surrounded by his family and leaders from Congress.

# CHAPTER 1

# A Kid From Queens

Donald Trump is an American businessman. Over the years, he became one of the most powerful and well-known people in the United States. His career has included a number of high-profile, or attention-grabbing, businesses. He also became known as a television celebrity and an author. In 2016, Trump was elected president of the United States. He was the first person elected president who had never held a **political** office or a military command.

Trump has a star on the Hollywood Walk of Fame.

# Growing Up in New York

Donald John Trump was born on June 14, 1946, in Jamaica, Queens. Queens is one of the five **boroughs** that make up New York City. Donald's father, Fred Trump, was well known as a builder of apartment buildings in New York City. His mother, Mary MacLeod Trump, came to New York from Scotland as a teenager. Donald has three older siblings—Maryanne, Frederick Jr., and Elizabeth—and a younger brother named Robert.

Donald and his siblings pose for a family portrait. From left to right, they are Robert, Elizabeth, Frederick Jr., Donald, and Maryanne.

A young Donald pushes a wheelbarrow outside his house.

Donald's parents were strict and demanding. They expected their children to work hard and do well in life. As a child, Donald had a lot of energy. He did well in school, but his parents felt that he needed discipline. So, when Donald was 13, they sent him to a boarding school called the New York Military Academy. Students at a boarding school live at the school instead of at home.

Donald smiles in his uniform for a school picture.

## School Days

Donald did well at the academy. He earned good grades and made a lot of friends. By the time he graduated in 1964, he was one of the school's top athletes and a student leader.

Donald wanted to be part of his father's **real estate** business. He had already been working at the company's construction sites during his summer vacations from school.

First, however, Donald had to go to college. He enrolled in Fordham University in New York City. But after two years there, he decided he wanted a school with a stronger business program. So he transferred to the Wharton School of Finance and Commerce at the University of Pennsylvania. Wharton was one of the best business schools in the United States. Trump graduated from there in 1968. Now it was time to take a bigger role in the family business.

Fred Trump (left) welcomed his son into the business after Donald graduated from Wharton.

# CHAPTER 2

# Building Big

After graduating from Wharton, Donald started working for his father full-time. In 1971, Fred Trump turned the whole business over to Donald. Now in charge, Donald had plenty of big ideas. Fred Trump had built apartment buildings for middle-class families in the outer sections of New York City. Donald wanted to focus on high-profile building projects in the heart of the city.

 Trump has never smoked, drunk alcohol, or taken drugs.

# A Grand Project

In 1976, Donald Trump took on his first big building project in Manhattan. This borough is famous for being an economic and cultural center. Trump offered to renovate, or fix up, an old hotel called the Commodore. Once one of the fanciest hotels in New York City, the Commodore no longer made much money. Trump made a deal. His company, called the Trump Organization, bought the hotel together with the Hyatt Hotel chain. Then Trump's company remodeled the building.

Trump (left) goes over plans for renovations on the Commodore with a New York City official.

The result was the Grand Hyatt New York hotel. It was a beautiful, 25-story building made of stainless steel and bright windows. The hotel was a huge success.

People dine in a beautiful, glassed-in section of the Grand Hyatt New York hotel.

The Grand Hyatt project made Trump the most well-known builder in New York. He had even bigger ideas. His next project would be one of the most sensational buildings in New York City.

Ivana and Donald Trump pose for a picture in their living room in Manhattan in 1979.

# Family Life

In 1977, Trump married Ivana Zelnickova Winklmayr. Ivana immigrated to the United States from Czechoslovakia. She had been a model. In 1978, Trump made his wife a vice president in charge of design at his company. Ivana worked on the renovation of the Grand Hyatt. She would go on to work on future Trump projects as well.

The Trump family began to grow over the next few years. In 1977, Ivana gave birth to their first child, Donald Jr. Their daughter, Ivanka, was born in 1981, and their second son, Eric, was born in 1984. All three children would grow up to work in the Trump Organization.

Ivanka, Ivana, and Donald Jr.

# Trump Tower

Trump Tower is recognizable for its jagged exterior.

In 1979, Trump chose a site on Fifth Avenue next to the famous Tiffany jewelry store in Manhattan. This area is famous for being expensive and stylish. There, Trump began his fanciest building project yet: Trump Tower. When it was finished, the building was 58 stories high with a shiny glass exterior.

The upper floors include luxury apartments, while the lower floors have businesses, restaurants, and stores. The lobby of Trump Tower is made of pink marble and has an 80-foot (24-meter) waterfall. The lobby is owned by New York City and is open to the public. One home for Trump and his family is located on the top three floors of the building.

Trump Tower's lobby is about 10 stories high.

# New York Real Estate

Trump's businesses in New York City continued to grow. He renovated an old hotel called the Barbizon Plaza and renamed it Trump Parc. In 1988, he bought the famous Plaza Hotel and put his wife, Ivana, in charge of renovating the building. As the years passed, Trump came to own more than a dozen New York City buildings. Most of them featured his favorite style: glass and steel.

One side of the Plaza Hotel looks out over New York City's Central Park.

# Wollman Rink

By 1980, the beloved Wollman ice-skating rink in New York City's Central Park was falling apart. It was closed. City officials worked to repair it, but their efforts experienced many delays. Then, in 1986, Donald Trump offered to rebuild Wollman at no cost to the city. The rink reopened less than six months later. Trump got a lot of good publicity, and New Yorkers once again had a Central Park skating rink to enjoy.

Trump often puts his name on his buildings, including the Taj Mahal casino.

## Growing Businesses

During the 1980s, Trump expanded his interests outside of New York City. Early in the decade, he bought land for his first **casino** in Atlantic City, New Jersey. It opened as Trump Plaza in 1982. By 1990, Trump owned three casinos in Atlantic City. They included Taj Mahal, then the largest casino in the world.

Trump loved to play golf. Over the years, he built or acquired golf courses all over the world. They are scattered from Scotland to Dubai and Florida to New York State. His business also grew to include hotels and country clubs. One of his most famous clubs is the Mar-a-Lago resort in Florida. Trump and his family sometimes live there. The property is also available to wealthy guests.

Mar-a-Lago translates to "Sea-to-Lake" in Spanish.

# Trouble in Paradise

By the late 1980s, Trump was famous around the world. Many people admired his ability to run so many successful businesses. He wrote popular books, and his name seemed to be in the news all the time.

However, real estate businesses across the United States weakened in the early 1990s. Trump's personal net worth dropped from $1.7 billion to $500 million.

# Timeline of Important Moments

**June 14, 1946**

Donald John Trump is born.

**1971**

Trump takes over the Trump Organization.

**1979**

Construction begins on Trump's first big Manhattan project, the Grand Hyatt New York hotel. A location is also chosen for Trump Tower

The Trump Organization took out huge loans to keep running. Some of its businesses filed for **bankruptcy**. The Trump Organization also sold buildings and either part or whole ownership of some businesses.

Trump faced personal problems during this time as well. He and Ivana divorced in 1992. In 1993, Trump married Marla Maples. The couple had a daughter named Tiffany. However, Trump and Maples divorced in 1999.

**2004**
The first season of *The Apprentice* airs on television.

**November 8, 2016**
U.S. voters elect Trump president.

**January 20, 2017**
Trump is sworn in as the 45th U.S. president.

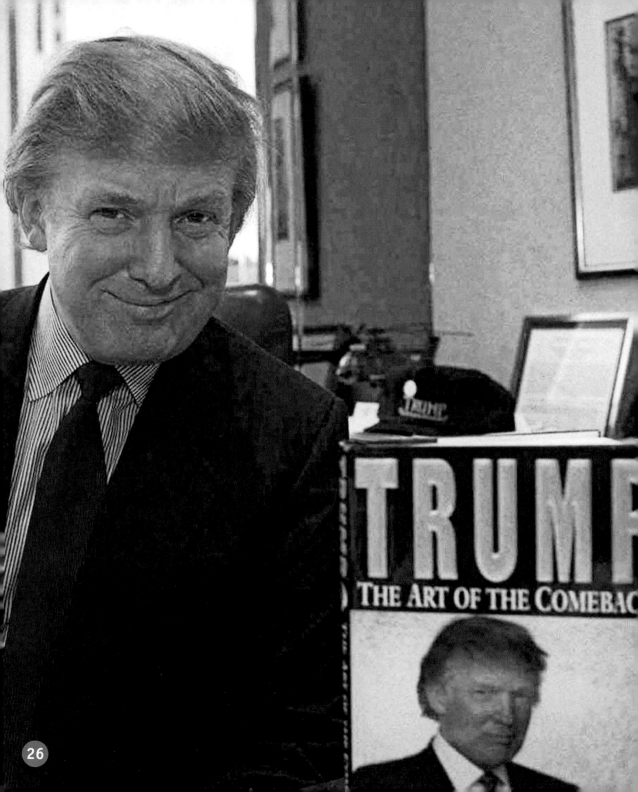

# Television Star

Trump's businesses were in trouble in the early 1990s. However, he began to work his way to success again in just a few years. Trump was proud of himself for being able to rise to the top of the business world again. He would later use this experience as a selling point when he ran for president.

In 1997, Trump cowrote a book about his return to billionaire status.

# Trump's TV Universe

By the late 1990s, Trump's business had expanded into television. In 1996, he became the owner of the Miss Universe, Miss USA, and Miss Teen USA beauty **pageants**. These competitions are aired on television. Trump owned the pageants for almost 20 years. He finally sold them in 2015.

Trump places a crown on Justine Pasek from Panama, who won Miss Universe in 2002.

"You're fired" became a popular catchphrase for Trump.

By the early 2000s, Trump did even more to bring his name to television. In 2004, he became the host of a TV show called *The Apprentice*. The show featured people trying to win a job with the Trump Organization. Contestants had to complete a different business challenge each week. At the end of each episode, the contestants would gather in Trump Tower for a meeting. Trump would tell the losing contestant, "You're fired!"

Trump sits with the 2014 cast of *Celebrity Apprentice*.

*The Apprentice* ran until 2007, and it was very popular. In 2008, the show changed to *Celebrity Apprentice*. This time, teams of famous people competed. Instead of winning a job with the Trump Organization, the celebrities competed for donations to a charity of their choice. Once again, Trump decided who would win and who would be fired.

In 2005, Trump married for the third time. His new wife was Melania Knauss. Knauss was a model who was born in Slovenia in central Europe. She came to the United States in 1996. In 2006, the Trumps welcomed their son, Barron.

Over the next 10 years, Trump continued to find success in business. However, his next move took many people by surprise. It was his most daring gamble yet.

Donald and Melania Trump pose for a photo with their son, Barron, in 2007.

# CHAPTER 4

# Trump for President!

Trump had become incredibly famous. As early as the late 1980s, some fans began saying he should run for president. Trump liked the idea. In 1999, he declared he would be the presidential **candidate** for a small political **party** called the Reform Party. However, by February 2000, he changed his mind and dropped out of the race. Then in 2015, Trump decided it was time to run again.

"The Donald" is a popular nickname for Trump.

# Many Candidates

On June 16, 2015, Trump announced he wanted to run for president of the United States. He would be part of the Republican Party, one of the United States' two biggest political parties. He gave a speech at Trump Tower to explain the issues he felt were important. Among the most important were ending illegal immigration, bringing jobs back to the United States, and fighting terrorism. Trump's slogan, or motto, was "Make America Great Again."

The Trump family stands together for pictures after Donald Trump's 2015 announcement that he was running for president.

Trump shakes hands with supporters during his campaign.

Many people were shocked at the idea of Trump as president. He had no political experience. He had never held a **public office** or taken part in political activities. For this reason, some people thought he was not qualified to be president. Others loved the idea of an outsider coming in to shake up the way the government was run. Some supporters felt ignored or neglected by the government. They believed Trump would look out for them.

Before he could run for president, Trump had to gain the Republican **nomination**. To do this, he had to win the primaries. These state elections help choose which individual will run for a political party. Sixteen other Republican candidates competed for the nomination. From the beginning, Trump had the most support from the public. During debates, his forceful answers caught people's attention. One by one, the other candidates dropped out. The Republican Party officially nominated Trump as its candidate on July 21, 2016.

Trump (left) argues with another Republican presidential candidate, Texas senator Ted Cruz, during a debate.

Supporters cheer for Hillary Clinton during a campaign speech.

Clinton's husband, Bill Clinton, was U.S. president from 1993 to 2001.

Trump ran against the Democratic Party's candidate, Hillary Clinton. Clinton was a strong choice for president. She had served as a New York State senator from 2001 to 2009. She was also secretary of state under President Barack Obama from 2009 to 2013. As secretary of state, she was the president's main adviser on international issues. However, many people did not like Clinton. They felt she was not trustworthy and would not bring enough changes to the government.

On November 8, 2016, millions of Americans went to the polls. Most people expected Hillary Clinton to win easily. However, it soon became clear that the race was close—very close. As the night went on, Trump took the lead and held it. Finally, early in the morning of November 9, the official word came. The next president of the United States would be Donald Trump!

A resident of Utah casts her vote during the 2016 presidential election.

# Campaign Statements

Trump made several statements during his campaign that were concerning to some people. For example, he promised to build a wall between the United States and Mexico to keep out illegal immigrants. Opponents argued that the cost and terrain made building the wall challenging. Others worried that Trump would **discriminate** against Muslims in his fight against terrorism. Some of Trump's critics felt he did not speak out against **prejudicial** people and groups strongly enough.

# Counting the Vote

Does the candidate who receives the most votes win? Not necessarily. The total number of votes a candidate receives is called the popular vote. U.S. presidents are not elected by popular vote. Instead, members of the Electoral College, called electors, choose.

Each state has a certain number of electors. This number equals how many representatives the state has in the U.S. Congress. There are a total of 538 electors.

Washington 12

Oregon 7

Montana 3

North Dak 3

Idaho 4

South Dak 3

Wyoming 3

Nevada 6

Nebra 5

Utah 6

Colorado 9

California 55

Arizona 11

New Mexico 5

Okla

Texas 38

Alaska 3

Hawaii 4

| Electoral Votes | |
| --- | --- |
| Trump | 306 |
| Clinton | 232 |

| Popular Votes | |
| --- | --- |
| Trump | 62,979,879 |
| Clinton | 65,844,954 |
| Other | 7,804,203 |

# 2016 Election Results

New Hampshire, 4
Vermont, 3
Massachusetts, 11
Connecticut, 7
New York, 29
Rhode Island, 4
New Jersey, 14
Delaware, 3
Maryland, 10
Washington DC, 3
Maine, 1
Maine, 3
esota
Wisconsin 10
Michigan 16
Iowa 6
Pennsylvania 20
Ohio 18
Illinois 20
Indiana 11
West Virginia 5
Virginia 13
Missouri 10
Kentucky 8
North Carolina 15
Tennessee 11
South Carolina 9
Arkansas 6
Mississippi 6
Alabama 9
Georgia 16
Louisiana 8
Florida 29

**KEY**
**Who Won the Electoral Vote?**
■ Republican, Donald Trump
■ Democrat, Hillary Clinton

A candidate needs 270 electoral votes to win.

Most states use a "winner takes all" approach to assign electoral votes. For example, New York has 29 electoral votes. The candidate who wins the popular vote in New York claims all 29 electoral votes.

A candidate can win the popular vote and still lose the presidency. In 2016, Clinton won the nation's popular vote. But Trump won the electoral vote.

Voters and children cheer for Trump on election night.

# Into the Presidency

Trump's election divided the country. Many people were upset that he won. They worried that Trump's presidency would be bad for minorities, immigrants, and other groups. They feared that people would become less tolerant of others. They also worried that the leaders of other countries would not want to work with Trump to make the world a safe place.

Other people were thrilled that Trump won the election. They believed he would make the United States stronger. They hoped his business experience would create more and better jobs for American workers.

At the beginning of his presidency in January 2017, the nation was full of expectation. It seemed likely that many big changes would happen in the next four years. ★

Trump takes the oath of office on January 20, 2017, becoming the 45th president of the United States.

**Number of brothers and sisters Donald Trump has:** 4

**Number of years Trump has run the Trump Organization:** More than 45

**Number of buildings Trump owns in New York City:** 13

**Number of children Trump has:** 5

**Number of votes Trump received in the primaries:** 13.3 million

**Number of electoral votes needed to win the presidency:** 270

**Number of electoral votes Trump won:** 306

**Donald Trump's net worth in 2016:** $3.7 billion

## Did you find the truth?

Trump's father was a real estate developer.

Trump ran for president of the United States for the first time in 2016.

# Resources

## Books

Marsh, Carole. *Donald Trump: America's 45th President*. Peachtree City, GA: Gallopade International, 2016.

Rall, Ted. *Trump: A Graphic Biography*. New York: Seven Stories Press, 2016.

Sherman, Jill. *Donald Trump: Outspoken Personality and President*. Minneapolis: Lerner Publishing Group, 2017.

Wooten, Sara McIntosh. *Donald Trump: From Real Estate to Reality TV*. Berkeley Heights, NJ: Enslow Publishers, 2008.

**Visit this Scholastic Web site for more information on President Donald Trump:**
★ www.factsfornow.scholastic.com
Enter the keywords **President Donald Trump**

# Important Words

**bankruptcy** (BANGK-ruhpt-see) a condition in which a person or company no longer has enough money to repay debts

**boroughs** (BUR-ohz) the five political divisions of New York City

**candidate** (KAN-di-dyt) a person who is running in an election

**casino** (kuh-SEE-noh) a building or room used for gambling

**discriminate** (dis-KRIM-uh-nate) to treat someone unfairly while you treat someone else better

**nomination** (nah-muh-NAY-shuhn) the suggestion that someone would be a good person to do an important job or receive an honor

**pageants** (PAJ-uhnts) a gathering of contestants at which judges select the most beautiful

**party** (PAR-tee) an organized group of people with similar political beliefs who sponsor candidates in elections

**political** (puh-LIH-tih-kul) of or having to do with governments and how they are run

**prejudicial** (prej-uh-DISH-uhl) having immovable, unreasonable, or unfair opinions about someone based on the person's race, religion, or other characteristic

**public office** (PUHB-lik AH-fihs) a position that involves a responsibility to the public, usually within the government

**real estate** (REEL ih-STATE) having to do with land and the buildings that are on it

# Index

Page numbers in **bold** indicate illustrations.

# About the Author

Joanne Mattern has written more than 250 books for children. She especially likes writing biographies because she loves to learn about real people and the things they do. Joanne also loves American history and thinks we are a very interesting nation! She grew up in New York State and still lives there with her husband, four children, and several pets.